Cool Sweet Muffins

Fun & Easy Baking Recipes for Kids!

Alex Kuskowski

Checkerboard
Library

An Imprint of Abdo Publishing
www.abdopublishing.com

visit us at www.abdopublishing.com

Published by Abdo Publishing, a division of ABDO, PO Box 398166, Minneapolis, Minnesota 55439. Copyright © 2015 by Abdo Consulting Group, Inc. International copyrights reserved in all countries. No part of this book may be reproduced in any form without written permission from the publisher. Checkerboard Library™ is a trademark and logo of Abdo Publishing.

Printed in the United States of America, North Mankato, Minnesota

062014

092014

THIS BOOK CONTAINS
RECYCLED MATERIALS

Editor: Karen Latchana Kenney
Content Developer: Nancy Tuminelly
Cover and Interior Design and Production:
Colleen Dolphin, Mighty Media, Inc.
Food Production: Frankie Tuminelly
Photo Credits: Colleen Dolphin, Shutterstock

The following manufacturers/names appearing in this book are trademarks: Anderson's®, Clear Value®, Gold Medal®, Kraft® Philadelphia®, Lunds & Byerly's®, Market Pantry®, Old Home®, PAM®, Roundy's®

Library of Congress Cataloging-in-Publication Data
Kuskowski, Alex, author.
  Cool sweet muffins: fun & easy baking recipes for kids! /
Alex Kuskowski.
    pages cm. -- (Cool cupcakes & muffins)
  Audience: 8-12.
  Includes index.
  ISBN 978-1-62403-304-9
  1. Muffins--Juvenile literature. I. Title.
  TX770.M83K873 2015
  641.8'157--dc23
                    2013043083

To Adult Helpers

Assist a budding chef by helping your child learn to cook. Children develop new skills, gain confidence, and make delicious food when they cook. Some recipes may be more difficult than others. Offer help and guidance to your child when needed. Encourage creativity with recipes. Creative cooking encourages children to think like real chefs.

Before getting started, have ground rules for using the kitchen, cooking tools, and ingredients. There should always be adult supervision when a sharp tool, oven, or stove is used. Be aware of the key symbols described on page 9. They alert you when certain things should be monitored.

Put on your apron. Taste their creations. Cheer on your new chef!

Contents

For the Love of Muffins!

Muffins are for more than just breakfast! Sweet muffins are a fun **dessert** you can take anywhere. They are also fun to make and eat.

The sweet muffins in this book are quick to make. They are easy to eat too. Muffins are the perfect grab-and-go snacks! Try each of the recipes in this book. Or get creative and make up your own!

This book has everything you need to get started. It's filled with fun recipes. Follow each recipe's easy steps to create tasty treats. Get inspired to create muffins that taste and look great!

The Basics

Ask Permission

Before you cook, ask **permission** to use the kitchen, cooking tools, and ingredients. If you'd like to do something yourself, say so! Just remember to be safe. If you would like help, ask for it! Always ask when you are using a stove or oven.

Be Prepared

→ Be organized. Knowing where everything is makes cooking safer and more fun!

→ Read the directions all the way through before starting the recipe. Remember to follow the directions in order.

→ The most important ingredient is preparation! Make sure you have everything you'll need.

Be Neat and Clean

→ Start with clean hands, clean tools, and a clean work surface.

→ Tie back long hair to keep it out of the food.

→ Wear comfortable clothing and roll up your sleeves.

→ Put on an apron if you have one. It'll keep your clothes clean.

Measuring

Many ingredients are measured by the cup, tablespoon, or teaspoon. Measuring tools may come in many sizes, but the amount they measure should be printed or **etched** on the sides of the tools. When measuring 1 cup, use the measuring cup marked 1 cup and fill it to the top.

Some ingredients are measured by weight in ounces or pounds. The weight is printed on the package label.

Be Smart, Be Safe

→ Never cook if you are home alone.

→ Always have an adult nearby for hot jobs, such as ones that use the oven or the stove.

→ Have an adult around when using a sharp tool, such as a knife or a **grater**. Always be careful when using these tools!

→ Remember to turn pot handles toward the back of the stove. That way you avoid accidentally knocking the pots over.

No Germs Allowed!

Raw eggs and raw meat have bacteria in them. These bacteria are killed when the food is cooked. But bacteria can survive on things the food touched and that can make you sick! After you handle raw eggs or meat, wash your hands, tools, and work surfaces with soap and water. Keep everything clean!

Cool Cooking Terms

Here are some basic cooking terms and actions that go with them. Whenever you need a reminder, just turn back to these pages.

Chop

Chop means to cut into small pieces.

Wash

Always wash fruits and vegetables well. Rinse them under cold water. Pat them dry with a **towel**. Then they won't slip when you cut them.

Whisk

Whisk means to beat quickly by hand with a whisk or a fork.

Mash

Mash means to press down on something with a fork or potato masher.

Symbols

Hot!

This recipe requires the use of a stove or oven. You will need adult **supervision** and assistance.

Sharp!

This recipe includes the use of a sharp **utensil** such as a knife or **grater**. Ask an adult to help out.

Kitchen Supplies

measuring cups

mini muffin tin

mixing bowls

measuring spoons

scoop

muffin
tin

paper
liners

zester

cutting
board

spatula

whisk

11

Ingredients

Here are some of the ingredients you will need:

maple syrup

yogurt

apple juice concentrate

whole milk

pumpkin puree

all-purpose flour

eggs

applesauce

mini chocolate chips

semi-sweet chocolate chips

non-stick cooking spray

lemons

bananas

unsalted butter

cream cheese

vegetable oil

strawberries

sour cream

vanilla extract

evaporated milk

Banana
Chocolate
Delight

Ingredients

2 ripe bananas
½ cup unsalted butter, softened
1¼ cups white sugar
2 eggs
1 teaspoon vanilla extract

1½ cups all-purpose flour
1 teaspoon baking soda
½ teaspoon cinnamon
¼ teaspoon salt
¾ cup mini-chocolate chips

Tools

2 muffin tins
paper liners
mixing bowls
fork

measuring cups & spoons
whisk
spatula
scoop

1   **Preheat** the oven to 350 degrees. Put paper liners in the muffin tins.

2   Put the bananas in a medium mixing bowl. Mash them with a fork.

3   Add the butter, sugar, eggs, and vanilla extract. Stir.

4   In a large bowl, whisk together the flour, baking soda, cinnamon, and salt.

5   Add the banana mixture to the flour mixture. Stir. Add the chocolate chips. Stir just enough to mix them in.

6   Divide the batter evenly between 18 muffin cups. Bake 25 minutes or until golden brown. Let the muffins cool.

Sweet Cinnamon Muffins

MAKES 24 SERVINGS

Ingredients

MUFFINS
non-stick cooking spray
2½ cups all-purpose flour
1½ teaspoons baking powder
½ teaspoon baking soda
¼ teaspoon salt
10 tablespoons unsalted butter, softened
1 cup white sugar
3 eggs
1½ teaspoons vanilla extract
1¼ cups sour cream

TOPPING
2¼ cups all-purpose flour
¾ cup brown sugar
2 teaspoons cinnamon
½ teaspoon salt
10 tablespoons unsalted butter, softened
2 cups powdered sugar
¼ cup whole milk

Tools

2 muffin tins
mixing bowls
measuring cups & spoons
whisk

spatula
scoop
spoon

1   **Preheat** the oven to 350 degrees. Grease the muffin tins with non-stick cooking spray. In a large mixing bowl, whisk together the flour, baking powder, baking soda, and salt.

2   In a medium bowl, whisk together the butter and sugar. Whisk in the eggs and vanilla extract. Add the butter mixture to the flour mixture. Stir with a spatula. Stir in the sour cream. Divide the batter evenly between the muffin cups.

3   Make the topping. Put the flour, brown sugar, cinnamon, salt, and butter in a medium bowl. Stir. Sprinkle the topping on the muffins. Bake 25 minutes. Let cool 10 minutes.

4   In a small bowl, whisk together the powdered sugar and milk. **Drizzle** it over the muffins with a spoon.

Perfect Cider Donut Pops

MAKES 24 SERVINGS

Ingredients

MUFFINS

non-stick cooking spray
¼ cup unsalted butter, softened
¼ cup applesauce
½ cup white sugar
⅓ cup brown sugar
3 tablespoons apple juice
   concentrate, thawed
2 eggs
1 teaspoon vanilla extract
1 cup whole milk

2⅔ cups all-purpose flour
1½ teaspoons baking powder
¼ teaspoon baking soda
¼ teaspoon nutmeg
1 teaspoon cinnamon
¾ teaspoon salt

TOPPING

¼ cup unsalted butter
1 teaspoon cinnamon
½ cup white sugar

Tools

mini muffin tin
mixing bowls
whisk
measuring cups & spoons

spatula
scoop
small microwave-safe bowl
small bowl

1   **Preheat** the oven to 375 degrees. Grease the muffin tin with non-stick cooking spray.

2   In a large mixing bowl, whisk together the butter, applesauce, sugars, and apple juice concentrate. Whisk in the eggs, vanilla extract, and milk.

3   In a medium bowl, whisk together the flour, baking powder, baking soda, nutmeg, cinnamon, and salt. Slowly add the flour mixture to the butter mixture. Stir with a spatula.

4   Fill the muffin cups three-fourths full of batter. Bake 15 minutes or until golden brown. Let the muffins cool 5 minutes.

5   Make the topping. Put the butter in a microwave-safe bowl. Melt it in the microwave. Put the cinnamon and sugar in a separate bowl. Stir. Dip the top of each muffin in the butter and then in the sugar mixture.

Dreamy
Chocolaty
Muffins

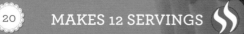

MAKES 12 SERVINGS

Ingredients

1⅛ cups all-purpose flour
½ cup unsweetened cocoa
    powder
¾ teaspoon baking soda
¼ teaspoon salt
½ cup white sugar
1 cup semi-sweet chocolate chips

½ cup unsalted butter, softened
2 eggs
½ cup yogurt
¼ cup whole milk
¼ cup vegetable oil
½ teaspoon vanilla extract

Tools

muffin tin
paper liners
mixing bowls
measuring cups & spoons

mixing spoon
whisk
scoop

1   **Preheat** the oven to 325 degrees. Put paper liners in the muffin tin.

2   Put the flour, cocoa powder, baking soda, salt, sugar, and chocolate chips in a large mixing bowl. Stir.

3   In a medium bowl, whisk together the butter, eggs, yogurt, milk, oil, and vanilla extract.

4   Add the butter mixture to the flour mixture. Stir.

5   Fill the muffin cups two-thirds full of batter. Bake 17 minutes. Let the muffins cool.

Ideal Poppy Seed Muffins

MAKES 12 SERVINGS

Ingredients

2 lemons
2 cups all-purpose flour
1 cup white sugar
2 teaspoons baking powder
¼ teaspoon baking soda
¼ teaspoon salt

¾ cup sour cream
2 eggs
1¼ teaspoons vanilla extract
½ cup unsalted butter, softened
2 tablespoons poppy seeds

Tools

muffin tin
paper liners
zester
mixing bowls
measuring cups & spoons

mixing spoon
sharp knife
cutting board
whisk
scoop

1   **Preheat** the oven to 400 degrees. Put paper liners in the muffin tin.

2   **Zest** the lemons into a large mixing bowl. Add the flour, sugar, baking powder, baking soda, and salt. Stir.

3   Put the sour cream, eggs, vanilla extract, and butter in a medium bowl. Stir.

4   Cut the lemons in half. Squeeze the juice into the sour cream mixture. Remove any seeds. Whisk until smooth.

5   Add the sour cream mixture to the flour mixture. Whisk in the poppy seeds.

6   Divide the batter evenly between the muffin cups. Bake 18 minutes or until the tops look golden. Let the muffins cool.

Sweet Strawberries 'n' Cream

MAKES 12 SERVINGS

Ingredients

non-stick cooking spray
4 oz. cream cheese
3 eggs
2 teaspoons vanilla extract
2 cups all-purpose flour
¾ cup white sugar

2½ teaspoons baking powder
½ teaspoon salt
½ cup unsalted butter, softened
1 cup whole milk
1 cup chopped strawberries
⅓ cup brown sugar

Tools

muffin tin
mixing bowls
mixing spoon

measuring cups & spoons
whisk
scoop

1   **Preheat** the oven to 400 degrees. Grease the muffin tin with non-stick cooking spray.

2   Put the cream cheese, 1 egg, and 1¼ teaspoons vanilla extract in a small mixing bowl. Stir.

3   In a large bowl, whisk together the flour, sugar, baking powder, and salt.

4   In a medium bowl, whisk together the butter, milk, 2 eggs, and remaining vanilla extract. Add the butter mixture to the flour mixture. Stir.

5   Fill each muffin cup halfway with batter. Add a layer of strawberries in each cup.

6   Add a teaspoon of the cream cheese mixture to each muffin cup. Then add 2 tablespoons of muffin batter to each muffin cup. Sprinkle extra strawberries and the brown sugar on top of the muffins. Bake 15 minutes. Let the muffins cool.

25

Mini Pancake Muffins

Ingredients

non-stick cooking spray
1 cup all-purpose flour
1 teaspoon baking powder
½ teaspoon baking soda
¼ teaspoon salt
2 tablespoons white sugar
⅔ cup plain yogurt

1 egg
2 tablespoons maple syrup
¼ teaspoon vanilla extract
2 tablespoons unsalted butter, softened
½ cup mini chocolate chips

Tools

mini muffin tin
mixing bowls
measuring cups & spoons
whisk

spoon
spatula
scoop

1   **Preheat** the oven to 350 degrees. Grease the muffin tin with non-stick cooking spray.

2   In a large mixing bowl, whisk together the flour, baking powder, baking soda, salt, and sugar.

3   Put the yogurt, egg, maple syrup, vanilla extract, and butter in a medium bowl. Stir.

4   Add the yogurt mixture to the flour mixture. Stir with a spatula. The batter should be slightly lumpy.

5   Gently stir in the chocolate chips. Fill the muffin cups two-thirds full of batter. Bake 9 minutes or until golden brown. Let the muffins cool 5 minutes. Serve with maple syrup for dipping.

Tip: Sweeten it up! Add more chocolate or peanut butter chips to the batter before baking!

Spicy Pumpkin Poppers

MAKES 24 SERVINGS

Ingredients

MUFFINS
non-stick cooking spray
1 cup all-purpose flour
¼ cup white sugar
¼ cup brown sugar
2 teaspoons baking powder
1½ teaspoons cinnamon
¼ teaspoon ground ginger
½ teaspoon nutmeg
½ teaspoon salt

1¼ cups pumpkin puree
¼ cup unsalted butter, softened
½ cup evaporated milk
1 egg
1½ teaspoons vanilla extract

TOPPING
2 tablespoons white sugar
1 teaspoon cinnamon
¼ teaspoon nutmeg

Tools

mini muffin tin
mixing bowls
measuring cups & spoons

spatula
scoop

1   **Preheat** the oven to 400 degrees. Grease the muffin tin with non-stick cooking spray.

2   Put the flour, sugars, baking powder, cinnamon, ginger, nutmeg, and salt in a large mixing bowl. Stir.

3   Put the pumpkin, butter, milk, egg, and vanilla extract in a medium bowl. Stir. Add the pumpkin mixture to the flour mixture. Stir with a spatula.

4   Fill the muffin cups halfway with batter.

5   Put the ingredients in a small bowl. Stir. Sprinkle the topping on top of the muffins. Bake 9 minutes. Let the muffins cool.

Tip: Try topping these muffins with melted chocolate or powdered sugar!

Conclusion

Sweet muffins are **delicious** and fun to eat. Making sweet muffins doesn't have to be hard. It can be easy and fun!

This book has tons of fun recipes to get you started. There's more to discover too. Check your local library for more muffin cookbooks. Or use your imagination and whip up your very own creations!

Make muffins for any occasion. Your friends and family will love tasting your freshly baked recipes. Become a muffin tin chef today!

Web Sites

To learn more about cool cooking, visit ABDO online at www.abdopublishing.com. Web sites about cool cooking are featured on our Book Links page. These links are monitored and updated to provide the most current information available.

Glossary

delicious – very pleasing to taste or smell.

dessert – a sweet food, such as fruit, ice cream, or pastry, served after a meal.

drizzle – to pour in a thin stream.

etch – to carve into something.

grater – a tool with rough-edged holes used to shred something into small pieces.

permission – when a person in charge says it's okay to do something.

preheat – to heat an oven to a certain temperature before putting in the food.

supervision – the act of watching over or directing others.

towel – a cloth or paper used for cleaning or drying.

utensil – a tool used to prepare or eat food.

zest – to lightly remove some of the peel from a citrus fruit using a zester.

Index

DATE DUE

			PRINTED IN U.S.A.